The glory of the last days

End time ethics

The glory
Of the
Last days

End time ethics

The glory

Of the

Last days

End time prophecies

End time ethics

The glory of the last days

By: Vusi Mxolisi Zitha

Copyright © 2020 Vusi Mxolisi Zitha

All rights reserved. No part of this publication may be reproduced, distributed or transmitted in any form or by any means, including photocopy, recording or other electronic methods, without the necessary written permission of the publisher. For permission request; write to the publisher at the address below.

ISBN: 9798600716483

Imprint: independently published

Write to:

Vusi Mxolisi Zitha

Po Box 324, Mzinti, 1352

Mpumalanga

South Africa

Email: vusimxolisi@gmail.com

All scripture quotations and or references if any; are taken

End time ethics

The glory of the last days

from GNT, NIV, and KJV version of the bible.

DEDICATION

To

All brethren's in Christ Jesus

End time ethics

The glory of the last days

CONTENTS

Chapter 1 signs of the end of the age

Chapter 2 the great tribulations

Chapter 3 the man of lawlessness

Chapter 4 difficult times ahead

Chapter 5 the day of the lord

Chapter 6 the coming of the son of man

Chapter 7 end time ethics

Chapter 8 waiting for the lord

Chapter 9 stand firm

Chapter 10 judgment

Chapter 11 the time is near

Chapter 12 the time of the end

End time ethics

The glory of the last days

End time ethics

PREFACE

On the last day only true believers shall be raptured. This book is a collection of bible verses about the end time warnings and prophecies. The bible tells us about the series of occasions that must transpire before the rapture; these series of events are referred to as "birth pains". Read as the events unfold, discern the time we are in and comprehend how close we are to the end.

INTRODUCTION

Jesus is coming again, when he comes; will you be ready for him. Don't wait for tomorrow to change your mind, if you haven't received him, accept him today as your lord and savior and live your life to his own satisfaction. The end of all things is now at hand, the house of Israel will soon be restored to its former state. Prepare for your soul, Jesus is lord and the one who is above is above all things. All things shall pass away and only his word will it remain forever.

Chapter 1

Signs of the End of the Age

MATHEW 24 VERSE 3 While He was sitting on the Mount of Olives, the disciples approached Him privately and said, "Tell us, when will these things happen? And what is the sign of Your coming and of the end of the age?"

Then Jesus replied to them: "Watch out that no one deceives you. For many will come in My name, saying, 'I am the Messiah,' and they will deceive many.

The glory of the last days

You are going to hear of wars and rumors of wars. See that you are not alarmed, because these things must take place, but the end is not yet. For nation will rise up against nation and kingdom against kingdom. There will be famines and earthquakes in various places. All these events are the beginning of birth pains.

It is now the generation that many who comes in the name of the lord, are not of him, it is the time that people uses the word of God to lure you into evil.

End time ethics

The glory of the last days

Even those who do not proclaim by mouth that they are the Messiah; shows it by their actions. It is your own responsibility to ensure that you are not enticed by their deceitful speech, for they are false in what they say and forgery in what they do. The whole world is pregnant and it will soon give birth to Jesus Christ again: the rumors of wars and wars are the beginning of labor pains. What is happening in the world is predestined to happen and it must surely take place.

End time ethics

Chapter 2

The Great Tribulation

MATHEW 24 VERSE 15 "So when you see the abomination that causes desolation, spoken of by the prophet Daniel, standing in the holy place" (let the reader understand), "then those in Judea must flee to the mountains! A man on the housetop must not come down to get things out of his house. And a man in the field must not go back to get his clothes.

Woe to pregnant women and nursing mothers in those days! Pray that your escape may not be in winter or on a Sabbath.

For at that time there will be great tribulation, the kind that hasn't taken place from the beginning of the world until now and never will again! Unless those days were limited, no one would survive. But those days will be limited because of the elect.

The glory of the last days

"If anyone tells you then, 'Look, here is the Messiah!' or, 'Over here!' do not believe it! False messiahs and false prophets will arise and perform great signs and wonders to lead astray, if possible, even the elect.

Take note: I have told you in advance. So if they tell you, 'Look, He's in the wilderness!' don't go out; 'Look, He's in the inner rooms!' do not believe it. For as the lightning comes from the east and flashes as far as the west, so will be the coming of the Son of Man.

End time ethics

The glory of the last days

Wherever the carcass is, there the vultures will gather.

As it is now in place that the house of the lord has become the burrow of harlots, it has become a refuge for imposter's, it has become a platform to exhibit abomination; it has become a safe less place to run to, wickedness dances on the pulpit and evil sit on the throne.

It has been said in advance that tribulation is bound to transpire, wickedness must take place.

The glory of the last days

We have seen, experienced and still to experience the sons and daughters of perdition, those who hide behind the scriptures, those who uses the word of God to cover their sins, those who operate darkness in the light, those who says "Jesus is Lord" with the lips of their mouth and says "Jesus be coursed " with the impurity of their heart.

They have risen (The false prophets), they are the true agents of Lucifer; they use the light to conceal darkness, They are true messengers of evil; they use signs and wonders to manipulate the righteousness of God, they are the true leaders of wickedness; they use the spirit of Antichrist to utter prophecies.

End time ethics

The glory of the last days

If the truth comes from a defiled source it becomes false, the good that comes as a results of evil is wickedness, nothing good comes from Satan.

His agents (the false Messiah) eats evil and vomit wickedness, they are the leaders of doom, watch them!! They preach the word and behave contrary to it; their actions always testify against them.

They are the authors of great tribulations and beside them is the devil who publishes it.

End time ethics

Jesus will not come on anyone's careful observation, nor at anyone's timing, follow his word; it is enduring, it is the righteousness of God, it is the one that leads to life. It is only a fool and a mad man that believes a mere man over what is said by Jesus.

Persecutions Predicted

MATHEW 24 VERSE 9 "Then they will hand you over for persecution, and they will kill you. You will be hated by all nations because of My name. Then many will take offense, betray one another and hate one another. Many false prophets will rise up and deceive many.

The glory of the last days

Because lawlessness will multiply, the love of many will grow cold. But the one who endures to the end will be delivered. This good news of the kingdom will be proclaimed in all the world as a testimony to all nations. And then the end will come.

It is the amount of tribulations, wickedness and the excessive buildup of lawlessness that determine the time we are in. indeed it is the Lord's glory of the latter days. where killing is the boldness of the heartless, where hatred triumph over love, and where you will be acquitted by your endurance.

End time ethics

Who so ever bears the name of Jesus must be prepared for hatred and persecution. Whoever wants to live peacefully and earn the heart of the world; will also face the consequences of his decisions.

Jesus said "lawlessness will multiply" which means there's and will be no solutions to these atrocities, wickedness will intensify and hatred will become the spheres of influence.

End time ethics

The glory of the last days

Betrayal will become the mode of living, and love a long lost friend of the heart. Falsehood will rule the nations and conspiracy will govern the parliaments. Injustice will be food of every nation. The only way out from these; is endurance.

The coming of Jesus will put an end the tribulations; Jesus will deliver those who endures until the end, those who fight for their faith, those without fast legs to commit what is evil, those who keep their tongue away from false utterances, and those who hold firm to their faith will not be moved nor swayed by the bitter words of the hypocrites.

End time ethics

The end of all things is here; the house that is not in order will be shattered, the soul that is defiled by immoralities will die forever. Prepare your own field; for the master is ready for the corn's harvest.

Chapter 3

The Man of Lawlessness

2THESALONIANS 2 VERSE 1 Now concerning the coming of our Lord Jesus Christ and our being gathered to Him: We ask you, brothers, not to be easily upset in mind or troubled, either by a spirit or by a message or by a letter as if from us, alleging that the Day of the Lord has come.

The glory of the last days

Don't let anyone deceive you in any way. For that day will not come unless the apostasy comes first and the man of lawlessness is revealed, the son of destruction.

He opposes and exalts himself above every so-called god or object of worship, so that he sits in God's sanctuary, publicizing that he himself is God.

Don't you remember that when I was still with you I told you about this? And you know what currently restrains him, so that he will be revealed in his time.

End time ethics

The glory of the last days

For the mystery of lawlessness is already at work, but the one now restraining will do so until he is out of the way, and then the lawless one will be revealed. The Lord Jesus will destroy him with the breath of His mouth and will bring him to nothing with the brightness of His coming.

The coming of the lawless one is based on Satan's working, with all kinds of false miracles, signs, and wonders, and with every unrighteous deception among those who are perishing.

End time ethics

The glory of the last days

They perish because they did not accept the love of the truth in order to be saved. For this reason God sends them a strong delusion so that they will believe what is false, so that all will be condemned — those who did not believe the truth but enjoyed unrighteousness.

The coming of Christ is the end of the age; if you are observant, you will see that the end is associated with "deception"; deception is a soul winning mechanism from the truthfulness of the Gospel to demonic teachings.

End time ethics

It is falling away from the truth, it is the spread of falseness in an attempt to overthrow the truth, it is to interpret the truth in a manipulative way and it is to conceal the truth with lie.

It is everyone's responsibility to examine all what is said and done in the light of God's word. Even though many may come in the name of the Lord, only few speak and act in the name of the Lord.

The glory of the last days

The man of lawlessness is the son of perdition, he suppress the truth to exalt lies, he consider evil the right thing to do, he says "there's nothing like sexual immorality; God said be fruitful and subdue the earth, he says " there's no offense in drinking; Jesus made wine himself for people to drink, he says "God is helpless without you helping him for your own good" he says abortion is the only key to unwanted pregnancies, he made prostitution an acceptable way of life. And nudity to be marketable.

End time ethics

These are the mysteries of lawlessness at work. Those who refuses to embrace the truthfulness of the Gospel; are enticed by the satanic methods of deception through false miracles, signs and wonders. When the devil is put to an end; his supporters and followers will not be spared.

Chapter 4

Difficult Times Ahead

2THIMOTY 3 VERSE 1 But know this: Difficult times will come in the last days. For people will be lovers of self, lovers of money, boastful, proud, blasphemers, disobedient to parents, ungrateful, unholy, unloving, irreconcilable, slanderers, without self-control, brutal, without love for what is good, traitors, reckless, conceited, lovers of pleasure rather than lovers of God, holding to the form of godliness but denying its power. Avoid these people!

For among them are those who worm their way into households and capture idle women burdened down with sins, led along by a variety of passions, always learning and never able to come to a knowledge of the truth.

Just as Jannes and Jambres resisted Moses, so these also resist the truth, men who are corrupt in mind, worthless in regard to the faith. But they will not make further progress, for their lack of understanding will be clear to all, as theirs was also.

The glory of the last days

Difficult times are true mark of the last days, it is where Satan takes hold of the hearts of those who are perishing, and making life too difficult for the righteous through the sins of the ungodly.

It is indeed the last hour; as we observed already people who conceal wickedness in the form of Godliness, those who put hope in the futility of their self-effort, those who betray their conscious by lying, and those who have much confidence in themselves and those who love with expectations.

End time ethics

These have all the devilish characters and always ready to act on a behalf of un-holiness. To be safe is to avoid these people; for you will fall victim of their recklessness, they are very corrupt in their thinking, they portray the truth to be bitter to win the hearts of those who are weak, they hold firm to blasphemy and always loyal in keeping their feet away from righteousness.

If you not careful; you will learn hatred from their misconducts, you will learn un-forgiveness from their grudges, you will learn disobedience from their deceitful words and you will learn to be ungrateful from their boastfulness.

People who follow the pleasures of this world love sin and they prove their sense of belonging. These are perilous times; those who have the spirit of fear have so much to lose, for what you fear is what you acknowledge as superior.

The devil will terrify you through the brutality of the ungodly, and through the signs and wonders of his lawlessness servants he will bring tremble. Only those with the spirit of boldness will survive the terror.

Chapter 5

The Day of the Lord 1

THESALONIANS 5 VERSE 1 About the times and the seasons: Brothers, you do not need anything to be written to you. For you yourselves know very well that the Day of the Lord will come just like a thief in the night.

The glory of the last days

When they say, "Peace and security," then sudden destruction comes on them, like labor pains come on a pregnant woman, and they will not escape. But you, brothers, are not in the dark, for this day to overtake you like a thief.

For you are all sons of light and sons of the day. We do not belong to the night or the darkness. So then, we must not sleep, like the rest, but we must stay awake and be serious.

End time ethics

The glory of the last days

For those who sleep, sleep at night, and those who get drunk are drunk at night. But since we belong to the day, we must be serious and put the armor of faith and love on our chests, and put on a helmet of the hope of salvation.

For God did not appoint us to wrath, but to obtain salvation through our Lord Jesus Christ, who died for us, so that whether we are awake or asleep, we will live together with Him. Therefore encourage one another and build each other up as you are already doing.

End time ethics

The glory of the last days

The day of the lord will not come on anyone's careful observation, the day and the hour is unknown, it will be a sudden destruction and only those who are in the dark will be overtaken by it, even those who think they can see beyond what they are looking at.

The children of God are the children of light and the children of light should be spiritually awake and serve the Lord whole heatedly with sincerity not lacking anything. Those who are still asleep are amongst the children of Satan and have nothing to do with light.

End time ethics

Be strong in faith, always keep your feet clean, be a bride ready for the bridegroom and hold on to his everlasting promises. Do not be deceived by mere words of the mere mortals, for they speak the revelations of their thoughts and prophesy the visions of their imaginations.

They quote the scriptures to justify sins, they question God's authority with words without insight and they use his word against him.

The glory of the last days

These are the sons of disaster; they that use salvation as a freedom to do evil, they manipulate the knowledge of God to meet their demands and always act against what they say. People who preach Christ for the sake of pound will always be there to entertain your heart desires and proclaim freedom where there's no bondage.

They will tell you what you want to hear and give you promises without fulfillment. Those who do so are setting up an appointment with God's wrath and those who follow their path will not be spared.

End time ethics

The Day of the Lord 2

2PETER 3 VERSE 1 Dear friends, this is now the second letter I have written to you; in both letters, I want to develop a genuine understanding with a reminder, so that you can remember the words previously spoken by the holy prophets and the command of our Lord and Savior given through your apostles.

First, be aware of this: Scoffers will come in the last days to scoff, living according to their own desires, saying, "Where is the promise of His coming? Ever since the fathers fell asleep, all things continue as they have been since the beginning of creation."

The glory of the last days

They willfully ignore this: Long ago the heavens and the earth were brought about from water and through water by the word of God. Through these waters the world of that time perished when it was flooded. But by the same word, the present heavens and earth are stored up for fire, being kept until the Day of Judgment and destruction of ungodly men.

End time ethics

The glory of the last days

The coming of Jesus has become a mock; it is now used in stand up comedies by those who live in ignorant; that his delay is associated with the pains he took through the beatings he suffered on the way to the cross.

Those who are perishing forget that by those stripes we are healed and Jesus is the word by which all things were created. The bible says in (2_peter 3 verse 9-18) 9 The Lord is not slow in keeping his promise, as some understand slowness. Instead he is patient with you, not wanting anyone to perish, but everyone to come to repentance.

End time ethics

The glory of the last days

10 But the day of the Lord will come like a thief. The heavens will disappear with a roar; the elements will be destroyed by fire, and the earth and everything done in it will be laid bare.

11 Since everything will be destroyed in this way, what kind of people ought you to be? You ought to live holy and godly lives 12 as you look forward to the day of God and speed its coming.

That day will bring about the destruction of the heavens by fire, and the elements will melt in the heat.

End time ethics

The glory of the last days

13 But in keeping with his promise we are looking forward to a new heaven and a new earth, where righteousness dwells.

14 So then, dear friends, since you are looking forward to this, make every effort to be found spotless, blameless and at peace with him.

15 Bear in mind that our Lord's patience means salvation, just as our dear brother Paul also wrote you with the wisdom that God gave him.

End time ethics

The glory of the last days

16 He writes the same way in all his letters, speaking in them of these matters. His letters contain some things that are hard to understand, which ignorant and unstable people distort, as they do the other Scriptures, to their own destruction.

17 Therefore, dear friends, since you have been forewarned, be on your guard so that you may not be carried away by the error of the lawless and fall from your secure position. 18 But grow in the grace and knowledge of our Lord and Savior Jesus Christ. To him be glory both now and forever! Amen. "

Chapter 6

End time ethics

The glory of the last days

The Coming of the Son of Man

MATHEW 24 VERSE 29"Immediately after the tribulation of those days:

The sun will be darkened,

And the moon will not shed its light;

The stars will fall from the sky,

And the celestial powers will be shaken.

"Then the sign of the Son of Man will appear in the sky, and then all the peoples of the earth will mourn; and they will see the Son of Man coming on the clouds of heaven with power and great glory. He will send out His angels with a loud trumpet, and they will gather His elect from the four winds, from one end of the sky to the other.

End time ethics

The glory of the last days

It will take days of great tribulations before our savior Jesus Christ appear. Those are the days of hard times, when incurable diseases and sicknesses surfaces, the days of newly born diseases without remedy.

More wickedness and heartlessness will descend across every nation, without remorse; people will kill and slaughter each other, the devil will spice up this world with fun more destructive than ever.

Many will become addicted to shedding blood, intoxicating substances will become the drive towards tragedy, many disturbing incidences will receive a wide spread television news, the world will become unsafe than ever before , peace will abdicate the throne and ruthlessness will be a new king.

Fear will be food to every nation and the weak will be eliminated. People whom you trust the most will look at you as an antelope as they become hungry hyenas. They will suppress the truth to victimize the innocent, they will say "come, join us and we will spare your life", they will be citizens of corruption and a sharp thorn in your flesh, be careful!!!, not to trust in your own strength to rescue yourself, for self-effort will be extremely futile.

Remember the words of Jesus "MATHEW 16 VERSE 24Then Jesus said to His disciples, "If anyone wants to come with Me, he must deny himself, take up his cross, and follow Me. For whoever wants to save his life will lose it, but whoever loses his life because of Me will find it.

The glory of the last days

What will it benefit a man if he gains the whole world yet loses his life? Or what will a man give in exchange for his life? For the Son of Man is going to come with His angels in the glory of His Father, and then He will reward each according to what he has done.

In the midst of those tribulations; only those who persevere until the end will be saved, but those who fail in strength will be destined to everlasting agony.

End time ethics

The glory of the last days

Many imposters who cover their darkness with the veil of light; will usher many into destruction in the name of Jesus and those without a descending spirit will fell prey to their predation. These are the people whom by their lips worship the Lord but with their heart far away from the truth that saves lives. Remember this " Mathew 7 verse 21 "Not everyone who says to me, 'Lord, Lord,' will enter the kingdom of heaven, but only the one who does the will of my Father who is in heaven.

End time ethics

The glory of the last days

22 Many will say to me on that day, 'Lord, Lord, did we not prophesy in your name and in your name drive out demons and in your name perform many miracles?' 23 Then I will tell them plainly, 'I never knew you. Away from me, you evildoers!'

They are all perpetrators of doom, their art of worship is abominable before God.

End time ethics

The glory of the last days

In these days; many are caged by alcohol and drunkenness is their lifestyles, stealing is their source of survival, they mock the truth by contrary acting on it, they walk the path of deceit and plot against the innocent. All these will be the birth pains of Jesus' return and the Lord's glory of the last days. After the great suffering; the signs of the lord Jesus will appear in the sky. By persevering till the end you will be saved, but by giving into temptations; you will be subject to judgment.

End time ethics

Chapter 7

End-Time Ethics

1PETER 4 VERSE 7 Now the end of all things is near; therefore, be serious and disciplined for prayer. Above all, maintain an intense love for each other, since love covers a multitude of sins.

Be hospitable to one another without complaining. Based on the gift each one has received; use it to serve others, as good managers of the varied grace of God.

The glory of the last days

If anyone speaks, it should be as one who speaks God's words; if anyone serves, it should be from the strength God provides, so that God may be glorified through Jesus Christ in everything. To Him belong the glory and the power forever and ever. Amen.

Since the end of all things is adjacent, you should be vigilant and discipline yourself through the Word of God in every sense of living, never despise prayer; do it always without ceasing, guard your tongue lest it get you into trouble, be strong in your faith and embrace love and extend it diligently to your fellow brethren's.

End time ethics

The glory of the last days

Fix your eyes on Christ; the author and the finisher of our faith, Do not drift away from the truth, hold firmly onto it, Do not live under the influences of your fleshly desires and the futility of your thoughts.

Pursue righteousness always. Never hold an offense against anyone, for this result in un-forgiveness and it is all the work of darkness. Immorality and impurity should not be mentioned amongst you, let God be your delight and watch out that you don't fall off from his grace.

End time ethics

The glory of the last days

May you always be joyful in your union with the Lord. I say it again: rejoice!

5 Show a gentle attitude toward everyone. The Lord is coming soon. 6 Don't worry about anything, but in all your prayers ask God for what you need, always asking him with a thankful heart. 7 And God's peace, which is far beyond human understanding, will keep your hearts and minds safe in union with Christ Jesus.

End time ethics

The glory of the last days

8 In conclusion, my friends fill your minds with those things that are good and that deserve praise: things that are true, noble, right, pure, lovely, and honorable. 9 Put into practice what you learned and received from me, both from my words and from my actions. And the God who gives us peace will be with you. (philipians 4 verse 4).

The glory of the last days

The Comfort of Christ's Coming

TESSALONIANS 4 VERSE 13 we do not want you to be uninformed, brothers, concerning those who are asleep, so that you will not grieve like the rest, who have no hope. Since we believe that Jesus died and rose again, in the same way God will bring with Him those who have fallen asleep through Jesus.

For we say this to you by a revelation from the Lord: We who are still alive at the Lord's coming will certainly have no advantage over those who have fallen asleep.

End time ethics

The glory of the last days

For the Lord Himself will descend from heaven with a shout, with the archangel's voice, and with the trumpet of God, and the dead in Christ will rise first. Then we who are still alive will be caught up together with them in the clouds to meet the Lord in the air and so we will always be with the Lord. Therefore encourage one another with these words.

The coming of Christ will be the comfort of believer's after a great tribulation from various incidences.

The glory of the last days

Only those who will persevere and overcome the pressures of life; will be given the right to eat on the tree of life. Those who are spiritually asleep will grieve on the day of the Lord.

To be asleep spiritually; is to be ignorant concerning the things of the spirit, is to serve the Lord without zeal,, it is to put confidence in the flesh, it is to seek for your own interest, it is to be prayer less and to be weak in faith.

The glory of the last days

Such people are not ready for Christ's return; they will not share from the great joy that awaits the Lord's righteous. Be awake, pull up your socks, time is not on anyone's side, destruction is coming like a thief in the night, befriend righteousness and remain attached to God's word.

For God said "Just be determined, be confident; and make sure that you obey the whole Law that my servant Moses gave you.

Do not neglect any part of it and you will succeed wherever you go.

8 Be sure that the book of the Law is always read in your worship. Study it day and night, and make sure that you obey everything written in it. Then you will be prosperous and successful. 9 Remember that I have commanded you to be determined and confident! Do not be afraid or discouraged, for I, the Lord your God, am with you wherever you go." (Joshua 1 verse 8).

Chapter 8

Waiting for the Lord

JAMES 5 VERSE 7 Therefore, brothers, be patient until the Lord's coming. See how the farmer waits for the precious fruit of the earth and is patient with it until it receives the early and the late rains. You also must be patient. Strengthen your hearts, because the Lord's coming is near.

The glory of the last days

Brothers, do not complain about one another, so that you will not be judged. Look, the judge stands at the door!

Brothers, take the prophets who spoke in the Lord's name as an example of suffering and patience. See, we count as blessed those who have endured. You have heard of Job's endurance and have seen the outcome from the Lord. The Lord is very compassionate and merciful.

End time ethics

No One Knows the Day or Hour

MATHEW 24 VERSE 36 "Now concerning that day and hour no one knows — neither the angels in heaven, nor the Son — except the Father only. As the days of Noah were, so the coming of the Son of Man will be. For in those days before the flood they were eating and drinking, marrying and giving in marriage, until the day Noah boarded the ark.

The glory of the last days

They didn't know until the flood came and swept them all away. So this is the way the coming of the Son of Man will be: Then two men will be in the field: one will be taken and the other left.

41 Two women will be grinding with a hand mill; one will be taken and the other left.

42 "Therefore keep watch, because you do not know on what day your Lord will come. 43 But understand this: If the owner of the house had known at what time of night the thief was coming, he would have kept watch and would not have let his house be broken into.

End time ethics

The glory of the last days

44 So you also must be ready, because the Son of Man will come at an hour when you do not expect him.

45 "Who then is the faithful and wise servant, whom the master has put in charge of the servants in his household to give them their food at the proper time? 46 It will be good for that servant whose master finds him doing so when he returns.

47 Truly I tell you, he will put him in charge of all his possessions.

End time ethics

The glory of the last days

48 But suppose that servant is wicked and says to himself, 'My master is staying away a long time,' 49 and he then begins to beat his fellow servants and to eat and drink with drunkards.

50 The master of that servant will come on a day when he does not expect him and at an hour he is not aware of. 51 He will cut him to pieces and assign him a place with the hypocrites, where there will be weeping and gnashing of teeth.

End time ethics

The glory of the last days

The Lord will come in the day and hour without your careful interpretations. So be faithful in all you do at all times, lest the day find you unprepared.

Do not let your happiness and enjoyment fool you, do not be blinded by riches and be deprived by poverty. keep watch of those who are pure in their lips but impure in their hearts, prepare yourself for the bride groom is yet to come, clothes yourself with white garments, and refrain from your wicked ways, for the path of wickedness leads to hell as a final destination.

End time ethics

The glory of the last days

But you! Be a faithful and a trusted servant,: not hypocrites who have a form of Godliness but denies its power, those who entice you with sweet words towards destruction, they are sheep's during the day but at night they transform into wolfs,

They say with their lips "Jesus be praised" and with their heart "Jesus be cursed". Such; they tie themselves with a belt of deceit and with their shoes; they are fast to run to evil, their tongue is more familiar with lies, they cover their darkness with white garments.

End time ethics

Do not be ignorant; acquire knowledge, and live life only to please God

Exhortations, warnings and blameless for the coming of the lord

THESALONIANS 5 VERSE 12 Now we ask you, brothers, to give recognition to those who labor among you and lead you in the Lord and admonish you, and to regard them very highly in love because of their work. Be at peace among yourselves. And we exhort you, brothers: warn those who are irresponsible, comfort the discouraged, help the weak, be patient with everyone.

End time ethics

The glory of the last days

See to it that no one repays evil for evil to anyone, but always pursue what is good for one another and for all.

Rejoice always!

Pray constantly.

Give thanks in everything,

for this is God's will for you in Christ Jesus.

Don't stifle the Spirit.

Don't despise prophecies, but test all things. Hold on to what is good. Stay away from every kind of evil.

End time ethics

The glory of the last days

Now may the God of peace Himself sanctify you completely. And may your spirit, soul, and body be kept sound and blameless for the coming of our Lord Jesus Christ. He who calls you is faithful, who also will do it.

Brothers, pray for us also. Greet all the brothers with a holy kiss. I charge you by the Lord that this letter be read to all the brothers. The grace of our Lord Jesus Christ be with you.

End time ethics

Chapter 9

Stand Firm

2THESALONIANS 2 VERSE 13 But we must always thank God for you, brothers loved by the Lord, because from the beginning God has chosen you for salvation through sanctification by the Spirit and through belief in the truth.

He called you to this through our gospel, so that you might obtain the glory of our Lord Jesus Christ.

The glory of the last days

Therefore, brothers, stand firm and hold to the traditions you were taught, either by our message or by our letter.

May our Lord Jesus Christ Himself and God our Father, who has loved us and given us eternal encouragement and good hope by grace, encourage your hearts and strengthen you in every good work and word.

End time ethics

The glory of the last days

Stand firm in faith through Christ Jesus, do not be moved by the winds of deceit, fight for your own salvation, do not be shaken by the forces of darkness, yes; the wrestle is not against flesh and blood but spiritual wickedness and the authorities of this world.

So hold on to what you received from him through faith so that you might obtain the glory of our savior Jesus Christ.

End time ethics

The glory of the last days

Be encouraged in your heart and be strengthen in your feet in every good work. Apostle Paul said "I urge you to live a life worthy of the calling you have received. 2 Be completely humble and gentle; be patient, bearing with one another in love.

3 Make every effort to keep the unity of the Spirit through the bond of peace. 4 There is one body and one Spirit, just as you were called to one hope when you were called; 5 one Lord, one faith, one baptism;

End time ethics

The glory of the last days

6 one God and Father of all, who is over all and through all and in all. (Ephesians 4 verse 1).But among you there must not be even a hint of sexual immorality, or of any kind of impurity, or of greed, because these are improper for God's holy people.

4 Nor should there be obscenity, foolish talk or coarse joking, which are out of place, but rather thanksgiving. 5 For of this you can be sure: No immoral, impure or greedy person—such a person is an idolater—has any inheritance in the kingdom of Christ and of God.

End time ethics

6 Let no one deceive you with empty words, for because of such things God's wrath comes on those who are disobedient. 7 Therefore do not be partners with them. (Ephesian 5 verse 3)

Chapter 10.

JUDGEMENT

God's Judgment and Glory

2THESALONIANS 1 VERSE 3 We must always thank God for you, brothers.

The glory of the last days

This is right, since your faith is flourishing and the love each one of you has for one another is increasing. Therefore, we ourselves boast about you among God's churches — about your endurance and faith in all the persecutions and afflictions you endure.

It is a clear evidence of God's righteous judgment that you will be counted worthy of God's kingdom, for which you also are suffering, since it is righteous for God to repay with affliction those who afflict you and to reward with rest you who are afflicted, along with us.

End time ethics

The glory of the last days

This will take place at the revelation of the Lord Jesus from heaven with His powerful angels, taking vengeance with flaming fire on those who don't know God and on those who don't obey the gospel of our Lord Jesus.

These will pay the penalty of eternal destruction from the Lord's presence and from His glorious strength in that day when He comes to be glorified by His saints and to be admired by all those who have believed, because our testimony among you was believed.

The glory of the last days

And in view of this, we always pray for you that our God will consider you worthy of His calling, and will, by His power, fulfill every desire for goodness and the work of faith, so that the name of our Lord Jesus will be glorified by you, and you by Him, according to the grace of our God and the Lord Jesus Christ.

The Last Hour

1 JOHN 2 VERSE 18 Children, it is the last hour. And as you have heard, "Antichrist is coming," even now many antichrists have come. We know from this that it is the last hour.

End time ethics

They went out from us, but they did not belong to us; for if they had belonged to us, they would have remained with us. However, they went out so that it might be made clear that none of them belongs to us.

But you have an anointing from the Holy One, and all of you have knowledge. I have not written to you because you don't know the truth, but because you do know it, and because no lie comes from the truth.

The glory of the last days

Who is the liar, if not the one who denies that Jesus is the Messiah? This one is the antichrist: the one who denies the Father and the Son. No one who denies the Son can have the Father; he who confesses the Son has the Father as well.

It is indeed the last hour; we have seen many falling away from the truth following demonic teachings. Some have backslides from the gospel of Jesus to establish their churches on the foundation of the Antichrist.

End time ethics

The glory of the last days

These are the false prophets, preachers and teachers who preach Christ in exchange for money, those who preaches the gospel of prosperity rather than salvation.

Many of you have lost focus on salvation and are too conscious of living a good life and to be prosperous in the land. Jude wrote in chapter 1 verse 1 "Dear friends, although I was very eager to write to you about the salvation we share, I felt compelled to write and urge you to contend for the faith that was once for all entrusted to God's holy people.

The glory of the last days

4 For certain individuals whose condemnation was written about long ago have secretly slipped in among you. They are ungodly people, who pervert the grace of our God into a license for immorality and deny Jesus Christ our only sovereign and Lord.

Confessing the coming of Jesus Christ in the flesh.

2JOHN 1 VERSE 7 Many deceivers have gone out into the world; they do not confess the coming of Jesus Christ in the flesh. This is the deceiver and the antichrist.

End time ethics

The glory of the last days

Watch yourselves so you don't lose what we have worked for, but that you may receive a full reward. Anyone who does not remain in Christ's teaching but goes beyond it, does not have God.

The one who remains in that teaching, this one has both the Father and the Son. If anyone comes to you and does not bring this teaching, do not receive him into your home, and don't say, "Welcome," to him; for the one who says, "Welcome," to him shares in his evil works.

End time ethics

The glory of the last days

Those who deceive you are not interested in what God is interested in, they cause division in the body of Christ, they persecute the truth to set lies free. They inspire you with words contrary to the words of Jesus Christ.

They would not tell you about the coming of our savior Jesus Christ, they concentrate your minds and hearts to materialistic things, what the devil wants you to know; that they will tell you and amongst themselves is a battle of spiritual powers.

End time ethics

The glory of the last days

The blind are enticed by their miraculous signs and wonders and through this; only the devil's wish is fulfilled. Follow Christ and not the man who stand in the position of Christ, they use their fake and useless powers to provoke your fears, they seek for their own interest, they do things in disobedience to God's word.

They say they are sent to liberate you from poverty and the yoke of Satan, they say they are sent for your breakthrough and they say God says "your time of suffering is over", that is how you know they are agents of Lucifer;

The glory of the last days

they have nothing to do with your salvation, they have nothing to do about your life after death, they teach you nothing about living righteously, they come as shield against your enemies, they say "send back an arrow to your enemies", they teach you to revenge, the battle is not yours but the Lord's.

How long will you continue to eat on the table of the enemy? How long will you disobey God to honor yourself? How long will you reject the truth to acknowledge lies?

End time ethics

The glory of the last days

How long will you consult the dead on the behalf of the living? How long will you acknowledge the truth in mind and deny it in actions? How long will you consider unrighteousness having fun?.
You are your own weapon of destruction, you cook your own evil and you shall eat it, you are too quick to hold onto lies and the truth shall judge you. Hold onto the teaching of Christ and Jesus must be honored in your life every day.

End time ethics

Chapter 11

The Time Is Near

REVELATION 22 VERSE 6 Then he said to me, "These words are faithful and true. And the Lord, the God of the spirits of the prophets, has sent His angel to show His slaves what must quickly take place."

"Look, I am coming quickly! The one who keeps the prophetic words of this book is blessed." I, John, am the one who heard and saw these things.

The glory of the last days

When I heard and saw them, I fell down to worship at the feet of the angel who had shown them to me. But he said to me, "Don't do that! I am a fellow slave with you, your brothers the prophets, and those who keep the words of this book.

Worship God." He also said to me, "Don't seal the prophetic words of this book, because the time is near. Let the unrighteous go on in unrighteousness; let the filthy go on being made filthy; let the righteous go on in righteousness; and let the holy go on being made holy."

End time ethics

The glory of the last days

"Look! I am coming quickly, and My reward is with Me to repay each person according to what he has done. I am the Alpha and the Omega, the First and the Last, the Beginning and the End.

"Blessed are those who wash their robes, so that they may have the right to the tree of life and may enter the city by the gates. Outside are the dogs, the sorcerers, the sexually immoral, the murderers, the idolaters, and everyone who loves and practices lying.

End time ethics

The glory of the last days

"I, Jesus, have sent My angel to attest these things to you for the churches. I am the Root and the Offspring of David, the Bright Morning Star."

Both the Spirit and the bride say, "Come!" Anyone who hears should say, "Come!" And the one who is thirsty should come. Whoever desires should take the living water as a gift. I testify to everyone who hears the prophetic words of this book: If anyone adds to them, God will add to him the plagues that are written in this book.

The glory of the last days

And if anyone takes away from the words of this prophetic book, God will take away his share of the tree of life and the holy city, written in this book.

He who testifies about these things says, "Yes, I am coming quickly."

Amen! Come, Lord Jesus!

The grace of the Lord Jesus be with all the saints. Amen.

End time ethics

The glory of the last days

Jesus gave these prophetic words and visions to his servant so that all the churches may know what is to take place and to prepare for the master's return. This book of revelation is the documentation of end time prophesies and visions.

It is the will of God that all the churches should know what is to take place and every church is supposed to read this book.

But in our days; the book of revelation is overlooked by many churches, to the extend that some even say the book of revelation is fearful.

End time ethics

The glory of the last days

If God only gives the spirit of boldness, it is no doubts that fear is directed from Satan.

If Jesus says "write this so that all the churches may know what will soon happen" and Churches neglect this; it simply means that only the purpose of Satan is served concerning the book of revelation.

Satan wants you to be ignorant of the truth, he wants you to pay attention to what is worthless, he wants to instill fear with regard to what will help you,

End time ethics

he wants you to be his disciple through disobeying the word, he hides important verses from you, he gives you his own interpretation of the scriptures, he decides for you when and when not to read the word, he chooses what to keep and what to overlook, he has become your usher spiritually.

Jesus is coming very soon, he has a reward in his hand; a reward of life to those who obey him and a reward of death to the disobedient.

The glory of the last days

Interpreting and moving with the times

Luke 12 verse 54 Jesus said to the crowd: "When you see a cloud rising in the west, immediately you say, 'It's going to rain,' and it does. 55 And when the south wind blows, you say, 'It's going to be hot,' and it is. 56 Hypocrites! You know how to interpret the appearance of the earth and the sky. How is it that you don't know how to interpret this present time?

End time ethics

The glory of the last days

Everything is bound to happen at a certain time with time at a certain place. As sons and daughters of heaven, you should not be ignorant of the times you are coming from and the times you are living in.

If you move with time, you will never be left behind of the happenings of this world. Those who are mindful of time, can interpret the current unfolding events.

End time ethics

The glory of the last days

We are now living and approaching that critical time where food will become the main source of illness, where the body will be very week against sickness and diseases.

It will not take a heavy illness to take one's life; but a mere headache, a stomachache and a common body pains will be enough to kill a person. Everything in your house will be a weapon to bring you destruction,

The glory of the last days

Wickedness will rise above the law that it cannot contend against it, the air you inhale and exhale will be polluted with chronic and contagious diseases, Spiritual blindness will descend across Christianity that those who serve God will be driven by their instinct and the revelations of their own imagination, and by this; more false leaders will rise to imitate Christ in a most deceitful way.

If you stay with God and move with time; nothing will happen without you knowing about it.

End time ethics

The glory of the last days

Your hearts will be under attack that you will display a negative attitude towards Christianity; many will Misquote God and Jesus to continue living in their transgressions. Love will be dethroned from the throne of the heart and hate will be the new king to rule over. Through king hate; the rumors of tragic death will spread across and many will live in fear as the world become more unsafe for its inhabitants. Satan will plant the seed of wickedness and our generation will produce evil as a result.

End time ethics

The glory of the last days

Be warned; Jesus is coming very soon, even 20 years from now is too soon for Jesus' return. The time left for his coming maybe too far for you, but as far as he is concerned every time is too soon for him. Blessed are those who hear the word of God and keep it.

End time ethics

The glory of the last days

Chapter 12

The Time of the End

DANIEL 12 VERSE 1 "At that time shall arise Michael, the great prince who has charge of your people. And there shall be a time of trouble; such as never has been since there was a nation till that time.

But at that time your people shall be delivered, everyone whose name shall be found written in the book. And many of those who sleep in the dust of the earth shall awake, some to everlasting life, and some to shame and everlasting contempt.

End time ethics

The glory of the last days

And those who are wise shall shine like the brightness of the sky above; and those who turn many to righteousness, like the stars forever and ever. But you, Daniel, shut up the words and seal the book, until the time of the end.

Many shall run to and fro, and knowledge shall increase." Then I, Daniel, looked, and behold, two others stood, one on this bank of the stream and one on that bank of the stream.

End time ethics

The glory of the last days

And someone said to the man clothed in linen, who was above the waters of the stream, "How long shall it be till the end of these wonders?" And I heard the man clothed in linen, who was above the waters of the stream; he raised his right hand and his left hand toward heaven and swore by him who lives forever that it would be for a time, times, and half a time, and that when the shattering of the power of the holy people comes to an end all these things would be finished.

End time ethics

The glory of the last days

I heard, but I did not understand. Then I said, "O my lord, what shall be the outcome of these things?" He said, "Go your way, Daniel, for the words are shut up and sealed until the time of the end. Many shall purify themselves and make themselves white and be refined, but the wicked shall act wickedly.

And none of the wicked shall understand, but those who are wise shall understand. And from the time that the regular burnt offering is taken away and the abomination that makes desolate is set up, there shall be 1,290 days. Blessed is he who waits and arrives at the 1,335 days. But go your way till the end. And you shall rest and shall stand in your allotted place at the end of the days.

End time ethics

The glory of the last days

The sins and doom of ungodly people

"3 My dear friends, I was doing my best to write to you about the salvation we share in common, when I felt the need of writing at once to encourage you to fight on for the faith which once and for all God has given to his people.

4 For some godless people have slipped in unnoticed among us, persons who distort the message about the grace of our God in order to excuse their immoral ways, and who reject Jesus Christ, our only Master and Lord.

End time ethics

The glory of the last days

Long ago the Scriptures predicted the condemnation they have received.

5 For even though you know all this, I want to remind you of how the Lord once rescued the people of Israel from Egypt, but afterward destroyed those who did not believe.

6 Remember the angels who did not stay within the limits of their proper authority, but abandoned their own dwelling place: they are bound with eternal chains in the darkness below, where God is keeping them for that great Day on which they will be condemned.

The glory of the last days

7 Remember Sodom and Gomorrah, and the nearby towns, whose people acted as those angels did and indulged in sexual immorality and perversion: they suffer the punishment of eternal fire as a plain warning to all.

8 In the same way also, these people have visions which make them sin against their own bodies; they despise God's authority and insult the glorious beings above.

End time ethics

9 Not even the chief angel Michael did this. In his quarrel with the Devil, when they argued about who would have the body of Moses, Michael did not dare condemn the Devil with insulting words, but said, "The Lord rebuke you!"

10 But these people attack with insults anything they do not understand; and those things that they know by instinct, like wild animals, are the very things that destroy them.

11 How terrible for them! They have followed the way that Cain took. For the sake of money they have given themselves over to the error that Balaam committed.

The glory of the last days

They have rebelled as Korah rebelled, and like him they are destroyed. 12 With their shameless carousing they are like dirty spots in your fellowship meals. They take care only of themselves.

They are like clouds carried along by the wind, but bringing no rain. They are like trees that bear no fruit, even in autumn, trees that have been pulled up by the roots and are completely dead.

13 They are like wild waves of the sea, with their shameful deeds showing up like foam. They are like wandering stars, for whom God has reserved a place forever in the deepest darkness.

End time ethics

The glory of the last days

14 It was Enoch, the seventh direct descendant from Adam, who long ago prophesied this about them: "The Lord will come with many thousands of his holy angels 15 to bring judgment on all, to condemn them all for the godless deeds they have performed and for all the terrible words that godless sinners have spoken against him!"

16 These people are always grumbling and blaming others; they follow their own evil desires; they brag about themselves and flatter others in order to get their own way.

End time ethics

The glory of the last days

Warnings and Instructions

17 But remember, my friends, what you were told in the past by the apostles of our Lord Jesus Christ. 18 They said to you, "When the last days come, people will appear who will make fun of you, people who follow their own godless desires."

19 These are the people who cause divisions, who are controlled by their natural desires, who do not have the Spirit. 20 But you, my friends, keep on building yourselves up on your most sacred faith. Pray in the power of the Holy Spirit,

End time ethics

The glory of the last days

21 and keep yourselves in the love of God, as you wait for our Lord Jesus Christ in his mercy to give you eternal life.

22 Show mercy toward those who have doubts; 23 save others by snatching them out of the fire; and to others show mercy mixed with fear, but hate their very clothes, stained by their sinful lusts.

End time ethics

The glory of the last days

A call to persevere

Perseverance is a mark of every true believer. Jesus said" be faithful even at the point of death, and he also said "whoever persevere these hard times till the end will be given authority to eat on the tree of life",. ....Therefore, among God's churches we boast about your perseverance and faith in all the persecutions and trials you are enduring. (2 Thessalonians 1 verse 4)......Not only so, but we also glory in our sufferings, because we know that suffering produces perseverance; 4 perseverance, character; and character, hope.

End time ethics

The glory of the last days

5 And hope does not put us to shame, because God's love has been poured out into our hearts through the Holy Spirit, who has been given to us. (Romans 5 verse 3). We have confidence in the Lord that you are doing and will continue to do the things we command. 5 May the Lord direct your hearts into God's love and Christ's perseverance. (2 Thessalonians 3 verse 5)

Surrounded by such a great cloud of witnesses, let us throw off everything that hinders and the sin that so easily entangles.

End time ethics

The glory of the last days

And let us run with perseverance the race marked out for us, 2 fixing our eyes on Jesus, the pioneer and perfecter of faith. For the joy set before him he endured the cross, scorning its shame, and sat down at the right hand of the throne of God.

3 Consider him who endured such opposition from sinners, so that you will not grow weary and lose heart. (Hebrews 12 verse 1).Consider it pure joy, my brothers and sisters, whenever you face trials of many kinds, 3 because you know that the testing of your faith produces perseverance.

End time ethics

4 Let perseverance finish its work so that you may be mature and complete, not lacking anything. (James 1 verse 3).

Brothers and sisters, as an example of patience in the face of suffering, take the prophets who spoke in the name of the Lord.

11 As you know, we count as blessed those who have persevered. You have heard of Job's perseverance and have seen what the Lord finally brought about. The Lord is full of compassion and mercy.

The glory of the last days

(James 5 verse 11)......... For this very reason, make every effort to add to your faith goodness; and to goodness, knowledge; 6 and to knowledge, self-control; and to self-control, perseverance; and to perseverance, godliness; 7 and to godliness, mutual affection; and to mutual affection, love. 8 For if you possess these qualities in increasing measure, they will keep you from being ineffective and unproductive in your knowledge of our Lord Jesus Christ.

End time ethics

9 But whoever does not have them is nearsighted and blind, forgetting that they have been cleansed from their past sins. (2peter 1 verse 6).

TO GOD BE THE GLORY

AMEN

ABOUT THE AUTHOR

Vusi Mxolisi Zitha is always been known by his virtue of honesty and integrity. His educational background in Nature Conservation includes writing of reports, articles and conducting field research. In 2009 he was involved in a Road Safety school debate under the motion: "Public transport and infrastructures are now ready for the 2010 FIFA world cup".

He got a certificate of achievement from the road safety department having been successfully defeating over nine schools contesting.
His scholastic contextual in nature conservation and debate has given him a

broad base from which to approach many topics.

Vusi has also served as a youth leader in the Church of God of Prophecy for over nine years. He also conducted several sermons and hosted youth services in the church as a junior pastor under the endorsement of District overseer Mr. Harry Mpumelelo Mavuso. His first book (Each step serves a purpose) is an inspirational, motivational and courageous book based on life encounters.

Other books by: Vusi Mxolisi Zitha

1. Each step serves a purpose

2. The realities of life

3. Exaltations to God

4. The book of proverbs

5. wise sayings

6. Eternity is the righteous only inheritance

7. Hell is the agony of the wicked

8. The glory of the last days

9. The book of parables

End time ethics

The glory of the last days

To get them type the book title on;

www.amazon.com

www.goodreads.com

www.smashwords.com

www.abebooks.com

www.kobowritinglife.com

www.powells.com

www.thriftbook.com

www.saxo.com

www.mightyape.co.nz

End time ethics

Connect with me on:

Social

https://m.facebook.com/vusi.mxolisi.75

https://www.instagram.com/vusi.mxolisi/

https://www.linkedin.com/in/vusi-mxolisi-zitha/

Web:

www.vusimxolisi.wordpress.com

http://vusimxolisi.tumblr.com/

Author page:

www.amazon.com//e/BO7YLVVW59

The glory of the last days

For quotes, sayings proverbs and inspirational stories

https://www.mirakee.com/vusimxolisizitha

https://www.yourquote.in/vusi-mxolisi-zitha-bqhjd/quotes

https://www.allchristianquotes.org/profile/user/2127/vusi_mxolisi_zitha/

https://www.wattpad.com/user/vusimxolisi

https://www.pinterest.com.mx/vusimxolisi/

For blogs

https://www.vusimxolisizitha.blogspot.com

https://www.goodreads.com/author_blog_posts/

https://www.vusimxolisi.wordpress.com/blog/

End time ethics

The glory of the last days

The glory of the last days

End time ethics

The glory of the last days

End time ethics

The glory of the last days

End time ethics

The glory
Of the
Last days

End time ethics

The glory

Of the

Last days

End time prophecies

The glory of the last days

By: Vusi Mxolisi Zitha

Copyright © 2020 Vusi Mxolisi Zitha

All rights reserved. No part of this publication may be reproduced, distributed or transmitted in any form or by any means, including photocopy, recording or other electronic methods, without the necessary written permission of the publisher. For permission request; write to the publisher at the address below.

ISBN: 9798600716483

Imprint: independently published

Write to:

Vusi Mxolisi Zitha

Po Box 324, Mzinti, 1352

Mpumalanga

South Africa

Email: vusimxolisi@gmail.com

All scripture quotations and or references if any; are taken

End time ethics

The glory of the last days

from GNT, NIV, and KJV version of the bible.

DEDICATION

To

All brethren's in Christ Jesus

End time ethics

The glory of the last days

CONTENTS

Chapter 1 signs of the end of the age

Chapter 2 the great tribulations

Chapter 3 the man of lawlessness

Chapter 4 difficult times ahead

Chapter 5 the day of the lord

Chapter 6 the coming of the son of man

Chapter 7 end time ethics

Chapter 8 waiting for the lord

Chapter 9 stand firm

Chapter 10 judgment

Chapter 11 the time is near

Chapter 12 the time of the end

End time ethics

The glory of the last days

End time ethics

PREFACE

On the last day only true believers shall be raptured. This book is a collection of bible verses about the end time warnings and prophecies. The bible tells us about the series of occasions that must transpire before the rapture; these series of events are referred to as "birth pains". Read as the events unfold, discern the time we are in and comprehend how close we are to the end.

INTRODUCTION

Jesus is coming again, when he comes; will you be ready for him. Don't wait for tomorrow to change your mind, if you haven't received him, accept him today as your lord and savior and live your life to his own satisfaction. The end of all things is now at hand, the house of Israel will soon be restored to its former state. Prepare for your soul, Jesus is lord and the one who is above is above all things. All things shall pass away and only his word will it remain forever.

Chapter 1

Signs of the End of the Age

MATHEW 24 VERSE 3 While He was sitting on the Mount of Olives, the disciples approached Him privately and said, "Tell us, when will these things happen? And what is the sign of Your coming and of the end of the age?"

Then Jesus replied to them: "Watch out that no one deceives you. For many will come in My name, saying, 'I am the Messiah,' and they will deceive many.

The glory of the last days

You are going to hear of wars and rumors of wars. See that you are not alarmed, because these things must take place, but the end is not yet. For nation will rise up against nation and kingdom against kingdom. There will be famines and earthquakes in various places. All these events are the beginning of birth pains.

It is now the generation that many who comes in the name of the lord, are not of him, it is the time that people uses the word of God to lure you into evil.

End time ethics

The glory of the last days

Even those who do not proclaim by mouth that they are the Messiah; shows it by their actions. It is your own responsibility to ensure that you are not enticed by their deceitful speech, for they are false in what they say and forgery in what they do. The whole world is pregnant and it will soon give birth to Jesus Christ again: the rumors of wars and wars are the beginning of labor pains. What is happening in the world is predestined to happen and it must surely take place.

End time ethics

Chapter 2

The Great Tribulation

MATHEW 24 VERSE 15 "So when you see the abomination that causes desolation, spoken of by the prophet Daniel, standing in the holy place" (let the reader understand), "then those in Judea must flee to the mountains! A man on the housetop must not come down to get things out of his house. And a man in the field must not go back to get his clothes.

Woe to pregnant women and nursing mothers in those days! Pray that your escape may not be in winter or on a Sabbath.

For at that time there will be great tribulation, the kind that hasn't taken place from the beginning of the world until now and never will again! Unless those days were limited, no one would survive. But those days will be limited because of the elect.

The glory of the last days

"If anyone tells you then, 'Look, here is the Messiah!' or, 'Over here!' do not believe it! False messiahs and false prophets will arise and perform great signs and wonders to lead astray, if possible, even the elect.

Take note: I have told you in advance. So if they tell you, 'Look, He's in the wilderness!' don't go out; 'Look, He's in the inner rooms!' do not believe it. For as the lightning comes from the east and flashes as far as the west, so will be the coming of the Son of Man.

End time ethics

Wherever the carcass is, there the vultures will gather.

As it is now in place that the house of the lord has become the burrow of harlots, it has become a refuge for imposter's, it has become a platform to exhibit abomination; it has become a safe less place to run to, wickedness dances on the pulpit and evil sit on the throne.

It has been said in advance that tribulation is bound to transpire, wickedness must take place.

The glory of the last days

We have seen, experienced and still to experience the sons and daughters of perdition, those who hide behind the scriptures, those who uses the word of God to cover their sins, those who operate darkness in the light, those who says "Jesus is Lord" with the lips of their mouth and says "Jesus be coursed " with the impurity of their heart.

They have risen (The false prophets), they are the true agents of Lucifer; they use the light to conceal darkness, They are true messengers of evil; they use signs and wonders to manipulate the righteousness of God, they are the true leaders of wickedness; they use the spirit of Antichrist to utter prophecies.

End time ethics

If the truth comes from a defiled source it becomes false, the good that comes as a results of evil is wickedness, nothing good comes from Satan.

His agents (the false Messiah) eats evil and vomit wickedness, they are the leaders of doom, watch them!! They preach the word and behave contrary to it; their actions always testify against them.

They are the authors of great tribulations and beside them is the devil who publishes it.

Jesus will not come on anyone's careful observation, nor at anyone's timing, follow his word; it is enduring, it is the righteousness of God, it is the one that leads to life. It is only a fool and a mad man that believes a mere man over what is said by Jesus.

Persecutions Predicted

MATHEW 24 VERSE 9 "Then they will hand you over for persecution, and they will kill you. You will be hated by all nations because of My name. Then many will take offense, betray one another and hate one another. Many false prophets will rise up and deceive many.

The glory of the last days

Because lawlessness will multiply, the love of many will grow cold. But the one who endures to the end will be delivered. This good news of the kingdom will be proclaimed in all the world as a testimony to all nations. And then the end will come.

It is the amount of tribulations, wickedness and the excessive buildup of lawlessness that determine the time we are in. indeed it is the Lord's glory of the latter days. where killing is the boldness of the heartless, where hatred triumph over love, and where you will be acquitted by your endurance.

End time ethics

The glory of the last days

Who so ever bears the name of Jesus must be prepared for hatred and persecution. Whoever wants to live peacefully and earn the heart of the world; will also face the consequences of his decisions.

Jesus said "lawlessness will multiply" which means there's and will be no solutions to these atrocities, wickedness will intensify and hatred will become the spheres of influence.

End time ethics

Betrayal will become the mode of living, and love a long lost friend of the heart. Falsehood will rule the nations and conspiracy will govern the parliaments. Injustice will be food of every nation. The only way out from these; is endurance.

The coming of Jesus will put an end the tribulations; Jesus will deliver those who endures until the end, those who fight for their faith, those without fast legs to commit what is evil, those who keep their tongue away from false utterances, and those who hold firm to their faith will not be moved nor swayed by the bitter words of the hypocrites.

The end of all things is here; the house that is not in order will be shattered, the soul that is defiled by immoralities will die forever. Prepare your own field; for the master is ready for the corn's harvest.

Chapter 3

The Man of Lawlessness

2THESALONIANS 2 VERSE 1 Now concerning the coming of our Lord Jesus Christ and our being gathered to Him: We ask you, brothers, not to be easily upset in mind or troubled, either by a spirit or by a message or by a letter as if from us, alleging that the Day of the Lord has come.

The glory of the last days

Don't let anyone deceive you in any way. For that day will not come unless the apostasy comes first and the man of lawlessness is revealed, the son of destruction.

He opposes and exalts himself above every so-called god or object of worship, so that he sits in God's sanctuary, publicizing that he himself is God.

Don't you remember that when I was still with you I told you about this? And you know what currently restrains him, so that he will be revealed in his time.

End time ethics

The glory of the last days

For the mystery of lawlessness is already at work, but the one now restraining will do so until he is out of the way, and then the lawless one will be revealed. The Lord Jesus will destroy him with the breath of His mouth and will bring him to nothing with the brightness of His coming.

The coming of the lawless one is based on Satan's working, with all kinds of false miracles, signs, and wonders, and with every unrighteous deception among those who are perishing.

End time ethics

The glory of the last days

They perish because they did not accept the love of the truth in order to be saved. For this reason God sends them a strong delusion so that they will believe what is false, so that all will be condemned — those who did not believe the truth but enjoyed unrighteousness.

The coming of Christ is the end of the age; if you are observant, you will see that the end is associated with "deception"; deception is a soul winning mechanism from the truthfulness of the Gospel to demonic teachings.

It is falling away from the truth, it is the spread of falseness in an attempt to overthrow the truth, it is to interpret the truth in a manipulative way and it is to conceal the truth with lie.

It is everyone's responsibility to examine all what is said and done in the light of God's word. Even though many may come in the name of the Lord, only few speak and act in the name of the Lord.

The glory of the last days

The man of lawlessness is the son of perdition, he suppress the truth to exalt lies, he consider evil the right thing to do, he says "there's nothing like sexual immorality; God said be fruitful and subdue the earth, he says " there's no offense in drinking; Jesus made wine himself for people to drink, he says "God is helpless without you helping him for your own good" he says abortion is the only key to unwanted pregnancies, he made prostitution an acceptable way of life. And nudity to be marketable.

End time ethics

The glory of the last days

These are the mysteries of lawlessness at work. Those who refuses to embrace the truthfulness of the Gospel; are enticed by the satanic methods of deception through false miracles, signs and wonders. When the devil is put to an end; his supporters and followers will not be spared.

End time ethics

Chapter 4

Difficult Times Ahead

2THIMOTY 3 VERSE 1 But know this: Difficult times will come in the last days. For people will be lovers of self, lovers of money, boastful, proud, blasphemers, disobedient to parents, ungrateful, unholy, unloving, irreconcilable, slanderers, without self-control, brutal, without love for what is good, traitors, reckless, conceited, lovers of pleasure rather than lovers of God, holding to the form of godliness but denying its power. Avoid these people!

The glory of the last days

For among them are those who worm their way into households and capture idle women burdened down with sins, led along by a variety of passions, always learning and never able to come to a knowledge of the truth.

Just as Jannes and Jambres resisted Moses, so these also resist the truth, men who are corrupt in mind, worthless in regard to the faith. But they will not make further progress, for their lack of understanding will be clear to all, as theirs was also.

End time ethics

Difficult times are true mark of the last days, it is where Satan takes hold of the hearts of those who are perishing, and making life too difficult for the righteous through the sins of the ungodly.

It is indeed the last hour; as we observed already people who conceal wickedness in the form of Godliness, those who put hope in the futility of their self-effort, those who betray their conscious by lying, and those who have much confidence in themselves and those who love with expectations.

The glory of the last days

These have all the devilish characters and always ready to act on a behalf of un-holiness. To be safe is to avoid these people; for you will fall victim of their recklessness, they are very corrupt in their thinking, they portray the truth to be bitter to win the hearts of those who are weak, they hold firm to blasphemy and always loyal in keeping their feet away from righteousness.

End time ethics

The glory of the last days

If you not careful; you will learn hatred from their misconducts, you will learn un-forgiveness from their grudges, you will learn disobedience from their deceitful words and you will learn to be ungrateful from their boastfulness.

People who follow the pleasures of this world love sin and they prove their sense of belonging. These are perilous times; those who have the spirit of fear have so much to lose, for what you fear is what you acknowledge as superior.

The devil will terrify you through the brutality of the ungodly, and through the

End time ethics

signs and wonders of his lawlessness servants he will bring tremble. Only those with the spirit of boldness will survive the terror.

Chapter 5

The Day of the Lord 1

THESALONIANS 5 VERSE 1 About the times and the seasons: Brothers, you do not need anything to be written to you. For you yourselves know very well that the Day of the Lord will come just like a thief in the night.

End time ethics

The glory of the last days

When they say, "Peace and security," then sudden destruction comes on them, like labor pains come on a pregnant woman, and they will not escape. But you, brothers, are not in the dark, for this day to overtake you like a thief.

For you are all sons of light and sons of the day. We do not belong to the night or the darkness. So then, we must not sleep, like the rest, but we must stay awake and be serious.

End time ethics

The glory of the last days

For those who sleep, sleep at night, and those who get drunk are drunk at night. But since we belong to the day, we must be serious and put the armor of faith and love on our chests, and put on a helmet of the hope of salvation.

For God did not appoint us to wrath, but to obtain salvation through our Lord Jesus Christ, who died for us, so that whether we are awake or asleep, we will live together with Him. Therefore encourage one another and build each other up as you are already doing.

End time ethics

The glory of the last days

The day of the lord will not come on anyone's careful observation, the day and the hour is unknown, it will be a sudden destruction and only those who are in the dark will be overtaken by it, even those who think they can see beyond what they are looking at.

The children of God are the children of light and the children of light should be spiritually awake and serve the Lord whole heatedly with sincerity not lacking anything. Those who are still asleep are amongst the children of Satan and have nothing to do with light.

End time ethics

The glory of the last days

Be strong in faith, always keep your feet clean, be a bride ready for the bridegroom and hold on to his everlasting promises. Do not be deceived by mere words of the mere mortals, for they speak the revelations of their thoughts and prophesy the visions of their imaginations.

They quote the scriptures to justify sins, they question God's authority with words without insight and they use his word against him.

End time ethics

The glory of the last days

These are the sons of disaster; they that use salvation as a freedom to do evil, they manipulate the knowledge of God to meet their demands and always act against what they say. People who preach Christ for the sake of pound will always be there to entertain your heart desires and proclaim freedom where there's no bondage.

They will tell you what you want to hear and give you promises without fulfillment. Those who do so are setting up an appointment with God's wrath and those who follow their path will not be spared.

End time ethics

The glory of the last days

The Day of the Lord 2

2PETER 3 VERSE 1 Dear friends, this is now the second letter I have written to you; in both letters, I want to develop a genuine understanding with a reminder, so that you can remember the words previously spoken by the holy prophets and the command of our Lord and Savior given through your apostles.

First, be aware of this: Scoffers will come in the last days to scoff, living according to their own desires, saying, "Where is the promise of His coming? Ever since the fathers fell asleep, all things continue as they have been since the beginning of creation."

End time ethics

The glory of the last days

They willfully ignore this: Long ago the heavens and the earth were brought about from water and through water by the word of God. Through these waters the world of that time perished when it was flooded. But by the same word, the present heavens and earth are stored up for fire, being kept until the Day of Judgment and destruction of ungodly men.

End time ethics

The glory of the last days

The coming of Jesus has become a mock; it is now used in stand up comedies by those who live in ignorant; that his delay is associated with the pains he took through the beatings he suffered on the way to the cross.

Those who are perishing forget that by those stripes we are healed and Jesus is the word by which all things were created. The bible says in (2_peter 3 verse 9-18) 9 The Lord is not slow in keeping his promise, as some understand slowness. Instead he is patient with you, not wanting anyone to perish, but everyone to come to repentance.

End time ethics

The glory of the last days

10 But the day of the Lord will come like a thief. The heavens will disappear with a roar; the elements will be destroyed by fire, and the earth and everything done in it will be laid bare.

11 Since everything will be destroyed in this way, what kind of people ought you to be? You ought to live holy and godly lives 12 as you look forward to the day of God and speed its coming.

That day will bring about the destruction of the heavens by fire, and the elements will melt in the heat.

End time ethics

The glory of the last days

13 But in keeping with his promise we are looking forward to a new heaven and a new earth, where righteousness dwells.

14 So then, dear friends, since you are looking forward to this, make every effort to be found spotless, blameless and at peace with him.

15 Bear in mind that our Lord's patience means salvation, just as our dear brother Paul also wrote you with the wisdom that God gave him.

End time ethics

The glory of the last days

16 He writes the same way in all his letters, speaking in them of these matters. His letters contain some things that are hard to understand, which ignorant and unstable people distort, as they do the other Scriptures, to their own destruction.

17 Therefore, dear friends, since you have been forewarned, be on your guard so that you may not be carried away by the error of the lawless and fall from your secure position. 18 But grow in the grace and knowledge of our Lord and Savior Jesus Christ. To him be glory both now and forever! Amen. "

Chapter 6

End time ethics

The glory of the last days

The Coming of the Son of Man

MATHEW 24 VERSE 29 "Immediately after the tribulation of those days:

The sun will be darkened,

And the moon will not shed its light;

The stars will fall from the sky,

And the celestial powers will be shaken.

"Then the sign of the Son of Man will appear in the sky, and then all the peoples of the earth will mourn; and they will see the Son of Man coming on the clouds of heaven with power and great glory. He will send out His angels with a loud trumpet, and they will gather His elect from the four winds, from one end of the sky to the other.

End time ethics

The glory of the last days

It will take days of great tribulations before our savior Jesus Christ appear. Those are the days of hard times, when incurable diseases and sicknesses surfaces, the days of newly born diseases without remedy.

More wickedness and heartlessness will descend across every nation, without remorse; people will kill and slaughter each other, the devil will spice up this world with fun more destructive than ever.

End time ethics

The glory of the last days

Many will become addicted to shedding blood, intoxicating substances will become the drive towards tragedy, many disturbing incidences will receive a wide spread television news, the world will become unsafe than ever before, peace will abdicate the throne and ruthlessness will be a new king.

Fear will be food to every nation and the weak will be eliminated. People whom you trust the most will look at you as an antelope as they become hungry hyenas. They will suppress the truth to victimize the innocent,

End time ethics

they will say "come, join us and we will spare your life", they will be citizens of corruption and a sharp thorn in your flesh, be careful!!!, not to trust in your own strength to rescue yourself, for self-effort will be extremely futile.

Remember the words of Jesus "MATHEW 16 VERSE 24 Then Jesus said to His disciples, "If anyone wants to come with Me, he must deny himself, take up his cross, and follow Me. For whoever wants to save his life will lose it, but whoever loses his life because of Me will find it.

The glory of the last days

What will it benefit a man if he gains the whole world yet loses his life? Or what will a man give in exchange for his life? For the Son of Man is going to come with His angels in the glory of His Father, and then He will reward each according to what he has done.

In the midst of those tribulations; only those who persevere until the end will be saved, but those who fail in strength will be destined to everlasting agony.

End time ethics

The glory of the last days

Many imposters who cover their darkness with the veil of light; will usher many into destruction in the name of Jesus and those without a descending spirit will fell prey to their predation. These are the people whom by their lips worship the Lord but with their heart far away from the truth that saves lives. Remember this " Mathew 7 verse 21 "Not everyone who says to me, 'Lord, Lord,' will enter the kingdom of heaven, but only the one who does the will of my Father who is in heaven.

The glory of the last days

22 Many will say to me on that day, 'Lord, Lord, did we not prophesy in your name and in your name drive out demons and in your name perform many miracles?' 23 Then I will tell them plainly, 'I never knew you. Away from me, you evildoers!'

They are all perpetrators of doom, their art of worship is abominable before God.

End time ethics

The glory of the last days

In these days; many are caged by alcohol and drunkenness is their lifestyles, stealing is their source of survival, they mock the truth by contrary acting on it, they walk the path of deceit and plot against the innocent. All these will be the birth pains of Jesus' return and the Lord's glory of the last days. After the great suffering; the signs of the lord Jesus will appear in the sky. By persevering till the end you will be saved, but by giving into temptations; you will be subject to judgment.

Chapter 7

End-Time Ethics

1PETER 4 VERSE 7 Now the end of all things is near; therefore, be serious and disciplined for prayer. Above all, maintain an intense love for each other, since love covers a multitude of sins.

Be hospitable to one another without complaining. Based on the gift each one has received; use it to serve others, as good managers of the varied grace of God.

The glory of the last days

If anyone speaks, it should be as one who speaks God's words; if anyone serves, it should be from the strength God provides, so that God may be glorified through Jesus Christ in everything. To Him belong the glory and the power forever and ever. Amen.

Since the end of all things is adjacent, you should be vigilant and discipline yourself through the Word of God in every sense of living, never despise prayer; do it always without ceasing, guard your tongue lest it get you into trouble, be strong in your faith and embrace love and extend it diligently to your fellow brethren's.

The glory of the last days

Fix your eyes on Christ; the author and the finisher of our faith, Do not drift away from the truth, hold firmly onto it, Do not live under the influences of your fleshly desires and the futility of your thoughts.

Pursue righteousness always. Never hold an offense against anyone, for this result in un-forgiveness and it is all the work of darkness. Immorality and impurity should not be mentioned amongst you, let God be your delight and watch out that you don't fall off from his grace.

The glory of the last days

May you always be joyful in your union with the Lord. I say it again: rejoice!

5 Show a gentle attitude toward everyone. The Lord is coming soon. 6 Don't worry about anything, but in all your prayers ask God for what you need, always asking him with a thankful heart. 7 And God's peace, which is far beyond human understanding, will keep your hearts and minds safe in union with Christ Jesus.

End time ethics

The glory of the last days

8 In conclusion, my friends fill your minds with those things that are good and that deserve praise: things that are true, noble, right, pure, lovely, and honorable. 9 Put into practice what you learned and received from me, both from my words and from my actions. And the God who gives us peace will be with you. (philipians 4 verse 4).

The glory of the last days

The Comfort of Christ's Coming

TESSALONIANS 4 VERSE 13 we do not want you to be uninformed, brothers, concerning those who are asleep, so that you will not grieve like the rest, who have no hope. Since we believe that Jesus died and rose again, in the same way God will bring with Him those who have fallen asleep through Jesus.

For we say this to you by a revelation from the Lord: We who are still alive at the Lord's coming will certainly have no advantage over those who have fallen asleep.

End time ethics

The glory of the last days

For the Lord Himself will descend from heaven with a shout, with the archangel's voice, and with the trumpet of God, and the dead in Christ will rise first. Then we who are still alive will be caught up together with them in the clouds to meet the Lord in the air and so we will always be with the Lord. Therefore encourage one another with these words.

The coming of Christ will be the comfort of believer's after a great tribulation from various incidences.

The glory of the last days

Only those who will persevere and overcome the pressures of life; will be given the right to eat on the tree of life. Those who are spiritually asleep will grieve on the day of the Lord.

To be asleep spiritually; is to be ignorant concerning the things of the spirit, is to serve the Lord without zeal,, it is to put confidence in the flesh, it is to seek for your own interest, it is to be prayer less and to be weak in faith.

The glory of the last days

Such people are not ready for Christ's return; they will not share from the great joy that awaits the Lord's righteous. Be awake, pull up your socks, time is not on anyone's side, destruction is coming like a thief in the night, befriend righteousness and remain attached to God's word.

For God said "Just be determined, be confident; and make sure that you obey the whole Law that my servant Moses gave you.

Do not neglect any part of it and you will succeed wherever you go.

8 Be sure that the book of the Law is always read in your worship. Study it day and night, and make sure that you obey everything written in it. Then you will be prosperous and successful. 9 Remember that I have commanded you to be determined and confident! Do not be afraid or discouraged, for I, the Lord your God, am with you wherever you go." (Joshua 1 verse 8).

Chapter 8

Waiting for the Lord

JAMES 5 VERSE 7 Therefore, brothers, be patient until the Lord's coming. See how the farmer waits for the precious fruit of the earth and is patient with it until it receives the early and the late rains. You also must be patient. Strengthen your hearts, because the Lord's coming is near.

The glory of the last days

Brothers, do not complain about one another, so that you will not be judged. Look, the judge stands at the door!

Brothers, take the prophets who spoke in the Lord's name as an example of suffering and patience. See, we count as blessed those who have endured. You have heard of Job's endurance and have seen the outcome from the Lord. The Lord is very compassionate and merciful.

End time ethics

No One Knows the Day or Hour

MATHEW 24 VERSE 36 "Now concerning that day and hour no one knows — neither the angels in heaven, nor the Son — except the Father only. As the days of Noah were, so the coming of the Son of Man will be. For in those days before the flood they were eating and drinking, marrying and giving in marriage, until the day Noah boarded the ark.

The glory of the last days

They didn't know until the flood came and swept them all away. So this is the way the coming of the Son of Man will be: Then two men will be in the field: one will be taken and the other left.

41 Two women will be grinding with a hand mill; one will be taken and the other left.

42 "Therefore keep watch, because you do not know on what day your Lord will come. 43 But understand this: If the owner of the house had known at what time of night the thief was coming, he would have kept watch and would not have let his house be broken into.

End time ethics

The glory of the last days

44 So you also must be ready, because the Son of Man will come at an hour when you do not expect him.

45 "Who then is the faithful and wise servant, whom the master has put in charge of the servants in his household to give them their food at the proper time? 46 It will be good for that servant whose master finds him doing so when he returns.

47 Truly I tell you, he will put him in charge of all his possessions.

End time ethics

The glory of the last days

48 But suppose that servant is wicked and says to himself, 'My master is staying away a long time,' 49 and he then begins to beat his fellow servants and to eat and drink with drunkards.

50 The master of that servant will come on a day when he does not expect him and at an hour he is not aware of. 51 He will cut him to pieces and assign him a place with the hypocrites, where there will be weeping and gnashing of teeth.

End time ethics

The glory of the last days

The Lord will come in the day and hour without your careful interpretations. So be faithful in all you do at all times, lest the day find you unprepared.

Do not let your happiness and enjoyment fool you, do not be blinded by riches and be deprived by poverty. keep watch of those who are pure in their lips but impure in their hearts, prepare yourself for the bride groom is yet to come, clothes yourself with white garments, and refrain from your wicked ways, for the path of wickedness leads to hell as a final destination.

End time ethics

The glory of the last days

But you! Be a faithful and a trusted servant,: not hypocrites who have a form of Godliness but denies its power, those who entice you with sweet words towards destruction, they are sheep's during the day but at night they transform into wolfs,

They say with their lips "Jesus be praised" and with their heart "Jesus be cursed". Such; they tie themselves with a belt of deceit and with their shoes; they are fast to run to evil, their tongue is more familiar with lies, they cover their darkness with white garments.

End time ethics

Do not be ignorant; acquire knowledge, and live life only to please God

Exhortations, warnings and blameless for the coming of the lord

THESALONIANS 5 VERSE 12 Now we ask you, brothers, to give recognition to those who labor among you and lead you in the Lord and admonish you, and to regard them very highly in love because of their work. Be at peace among yourselves. And we exhort you, brothers: warn those who are irresponsible, comfort the discouraged, help the weak, be patient with everyone.

The glory of the last days

See to it that no one repays evil for evil to anyone, but always pursue what is good for one another and for all.

Rejoice always!

Pray constantly.

Give thanks in everything,

for this is God's will for you in Christ Jesus.

Don't stifle the Spirit.

Don't despise prophecies, but test all things. Hold on to what is good. Stay away from every kind of evil.

End time ethics

The glory of the last days

Now may the God of peace Himself sanctify you completely. And may your spirit, soul, and body be kept sound and blameless for the coming of our Lord Jesus Christ. He who calls you is faithful, who also will do it.

Brothers, pray for us also. Greet all the brothers with a holy kiss. I charge you by the Lord that this letter be read to all the brothers. The grace of our Lord Jesus Christ be with you.

Chapter 9

Stand Firm

2THESALONIANS 2 VERSE 13 But we must always thank God for you, brothers loved by the Lord, because from the beginning God has chosen you for salvation through sanctification by the Spirit and through belief in the truth.

He called you to this through our gospel, so that you might obtain the glory of our Lord Jesus Christ.

The glory of the last days

Therefore, brothers, stand firm and hold to the traditions you were taught, either by our message or by our letter.

May our Lord Jesus Christ Himself and God our Father, who has loved us and given us eternal encouragement and good hope by grace, encourage your hearts and strengthen you in every good work and word.

End time ethics

The glory of the last days

Stand firm in faith through Christ Jesus, do not be moved by the winds of deceit, fight for your own salvation, do not be shaken by the forces of darkness, yes; the wrestle is not against flesh and blood but spiritual wickedness and the authorities of this world.

So hold on to what you received from him through faith so that you might obtain the glory of our savior Jesus Christ.

The glory of the last days

Be encouraged in your heart and be strengthen in your feet in every good work. Apostle Paul said "I urge you to live a life worthy of the calling you have received. 2 Be completely humble and gentle; be patient, bearing with one another in love.

3 Make every effort to keep the unity of the Spirit through the bond of peace. 4 There is one body and one Spirit, just as you were called to one hope when you were called; 5 one Lord, one faith, one baptism;

End time ethics

The glory of the last days

6 one God and Father of all, who is over all and through all and in all. (Ephesians 4 verse 1).But among you there must not be even a hint of sexual immorality, or of any kind of impurity, or of greed, because these are improper for God's holy people.

4 Nor should there be obscenity, foolish talk or coarse joking, which are out of place, but rather thanksgiving. 5 For of this you can be sure: No immoral, impure or greedy person—such a person is an idolater—has any inheritance in the kingdom of Christ and of God.

End time ethics

6 Let no one deceive you with empty words, for because of such things God's wrath comes on those who are disobedient. 7 Therefore do not be partners with them. (Ephesian 5 verse 3)

Chapter 10.

JUDGEMENT

God's Judgment and Glory

2THESALONIANS 1 VERSE 3 We must always thank God for you, brothers.

The glory of the last days

This is right, since your faith is flourishing and the love each one of you has for one another is increasing. Therefore, we ourselves boast about you among God's churches — about your endurance and faith in all the persecutions and afflictions you endure.

It is a clear evidence of God's righteous judgment that you will be counted worthy of God's kingdom, for which you also are suffering, since it is righteous for God to repay with affliction those who afflict you and to reward with rest you who are afflicted, along with us.

End time ethics

The glory of the last days

This will take place at the revelation of the Lord Jesus from heaven with His powerful angels, taking vengeance with flaming fire on those who don't know God and on those who don't obey the gospel of our Lord Jesus.

These will pay the penalty of eternal destruction from the Lord's presence and from His glorious strength in that day when He comes to be glorified by His saints and to be admired by all those who have believed, because our testimony among you was believed.

End time ethics

The glory of the last days

And in view of this, we always pray for you that our God will consider you worthy of His calling, and will, by His power, fulfill every desire for goodness and the work of faith, so that the name of our Lord Jesus will be glorified by you, and you by Him, according to the grace of our God and the Lord Jesus Christ.

The Last Hour

1 JOHN 2 VERSE 18 Children, it is the last hour. And as you have heard, "Antichrist is coming," even now many antichrists have come. We know from this that it is the last hour.

End time ethics

The glory of the last days

They went out from us, but they did not belong to us; for if they had belonged to us, they would have remained with us. However, they went out so that it might be made clear that none of them belongs to us.

But you have an anointing from the Holy One, and all of you have knowledge. I have not written to you because you don't know the truth, but because you do know it, and because no lie comes from the truth.

End time ethics

The glory of the last days

Who is the liar, if not the one who denies that Jesus is the Messiah? This one is the antichrist: the one who denies the Father and the Son. No one who denies the Son can have the Father; he who confesses the Son has the Father as well.

It is indeed the last hour; we have seen many falling away from the truth following demonic teachings. Some have backslides from the gospel of Jesus to establish their churches on the foundation of the Antichrist.

End time ethics

The glory of the last days

These are the false prophets, preachers and teachers who preach Christ in exchange for money, those who preaches the gospel of prosperity rather than salvation.

Many of you have lost focus on salvation and are too conscious of living a good life and to be prosperous in the land. Jude wrote in chapter 1 verse 1 "Dear friends, although I was very eager to write to you about the salvation we share, I felt compelled to write and urge you to contend for the faith that was once for all entrusted to God's holy people.

End time ethics

4 For certain individuals whose condemnation was written about long ago have secretly slipped in among you. They are ungodly people, who pervert the grace of our God into a license for immorality and deny Jesus Christ our only sovereign and Lord.

Confessing the coming of Jesus Christ in the flesh.

2JOHN 1 VERSE 7 Many deceivers have gone out into the world; they do not confess the coming of Jesus Christ in the flesh. This is the deceiver and the antichrist.

The glory of the last days

Watch yourselves so you don't lose what we have worked for, but that you may receive a full reward. Anyone who does not remain in Christ's teaching but goes beyond it, does not have God.

The one who remains in that teaching, this one has both the Father and the Son. If anyone comes to you and does not bring this teaching, do not receive him into your home, and don't say, "Welcome," to him; for the one who says, "Welcome," to him shares in his evil works.

End time ethics

The glory of the last days

Those who deceive you are not interested in what God is interested in, they cause division in the body of Christ, they persecute the truth to set lies free. They inspire you with words contrary to the words of Jesus Christ.

They would not tell you about the coming of our savior Jesus Christ, they concentrate your minds and hearts to materialistic things, what the devil wants you to know; that they will tell you and amongst themselves is a battle of spiritual powers.

End time ethics

The glory of the last days

The blind are enticed by their miraculous signs and wonders and through this; only the devil's wish is fulfilled. Follow Christ and not the man who stand in the position of Christ, they use their fake and useless powers to provoke your fears, they seek for their own interest, they do things in disobedience to God's word.

They say they are sent to liberate you from poverty and the yoke of Satan, they say they are sent for your breakthrough and they say God says "your time of suffering is over", that is how you know they are agents of Lucifer;

End time ethics

they have nothing to do with your salvation, they have nothing to do about your life after death, they teach you nothing about living righteously, they come as shield against your enemies, they say "send back an arrow to your enemies", they teach you to revenge, the battle is not yours but the Lord's.

How long will you continue to eat on the table of the enemy? How long will you disobey God to honor yourself? How long will you reject the truth to acknowledge lies?

The glory of the last days

How long will you consult the dead on the behalf of the living? How long will you acknowledge the truth in mind and deny it in actions? How long will you consider unrighteousness having fun?.

You are your own weapon of destruction, you cook your own evil and you shall eat it, you are too quick to hold onto lies and the truth shall judge you.

Hold onto the teaching of Christ and Jesus must be honored in your life every day.

End time ethics

Chapter 11

The Time Is Near

REVELATION 22 VERSE 6 Then he said to me, "These words are faithful and true. And the Lord, the God of the spirits of the prophets, has sent His angel to show His slaves what must quickly take place."

"Look, I am coming quickly! The one who keeps the prophetic words of this book is blessed." I, John, am the one who heard and saw these things.

The glory of the last days

When I heard and saw them, I fell down to worship at the feet of the angel who had shown them to me. But he said to me, "Don't do that! I am a fellow slave with you, your brothers the prophets, and those who keep the words of this book.

Worship God." He also said to me, "Don't seal the prophetic words of this book, because the time is near. Let the unrighteous go on in unrighteousness; let the filthy go on being made filthy; let the righteous go on in righteousness; and let the holy go on being made holy."

End time ethics

The glory of the last days

"Look! I am coming quickly, and My reward is with Me to repay each person according to what he has done. I am the Alpha and the Omega, the First and the Last, the Beginning and the End.

"Blessed are those who wash their robes, so that they may have the right to the tree of life and may enter the city by the gates. Outside are the dogs, the sorcerers, the sexually immoral, the murderers, the idolaters, and everyone who loves and practices lying.

The glory of the last days

"I, Jesus, have sent My angel to attest these things to you for the churches. I am the Root and the Offspring of David, the Bright Morning Star."

Both the Spirit and the bride say, "Come!" Anyone who hears should say, "Come!" And the one who is thirsty should come. Whoever desires should take the living water as a gift. I testify to everyone who hears the prophetic words of this book: If anyone adds to them, God will add to him the plagues that are written in this book.

End time ethics

The glory of the last days

And if anyone takes away from the words of this prophetic book, God will take away his share of the tree of life and the holy city, written in this book.

He who testifies about these things says, "Yes, I am coming quickly."

Amen! Come, Lord Jesus!

The grace of the Lord Jesus be with all the saints. Amen.

The glory of the last days

Jesus gave these prophetic words and visions to his servant so that all the churches may know what is to take place and to prepare for the master's return. This book of revelation is the documentation of end time prophesies and visions.

It is the will of God that all the churches should know what is to take place and every church is supposed to read this book.

But in our days; the book of revelation is overlooked by many churches, to the extend that some even say the book of revelation is fearful.

End time ethics

The glory of the last days

If God only gives the spirit of boldness, it is no doubts that fear is directed from Satan.

If Jesus says "write this so that all the churches may know what will soon happen" and Churches neglect this; it simply means that only the purpose of Satan is served concerning the book of revelation.

Satan wants you to be ignorant of the truth, he wants you to pay attention to what is worthless, he wants to instill fear with regard to what will help you,

End time ethics

The glory of the last days

he wants you to be his disciple through disobeying the word, he hides important verses from you, he gives you his own interpretation of the scriptures, he decides for you when and when not to read the word, he chooses what to keep and what to overlook, he has become your usher spiritually.

Jesus is coming very soon, he has a reward in his hand; a reward of life to those who obey him and a reward of death to the disobedient.

End time ethics

Interpreting and moving with the times

Luke 12 verse 54 Jesus said to the crowd: "When you see a cloud rising in the west, immediately you say, 'It's going to rain,' and it does. 55 And when the south wind blows, you say, 'It's going to be hot,' and it is. 56 Hypocrites! You know how to interpret the appearance of the earth and the sky. How is it that you don't know how to interpret this present time?

The glory of the last days

Everything is bound to happen at a certain time with time at a certain place. As sons and daughters of heaven, you should not be ignorant of the times you are coming from and the times you are living in.

If you move with time, you will never be left behind of the happenings of this world. Those who are mindful of time, can interpret the current unfolding events.

End time ethics

The glory of the last days

We are now living and approaching that critical time where food will become the main source of illness, where the body will be very week against sickness and diseases.

It will not take a heavy illness to take one's life; but a mere headache, a stomachache and a common body pains will be enough to kill a person. Everything in your house will be a weapon to bring you destruction,

End time ethics

The glory of the last days

Wickedness will rise above the law that it cannot contend against it, the air you inhale and exhale will be polluted with chronic and contagious diseases, Spiritual blindness will descend across Christianity that those who serve God will be driven by their instinct and the revelations of their own imagination, and by this; more false leaders will rise to imitate Christ in a most deceitful way.

If you stay with God and move with time; nothing will happen without you knowing about it.

End time ethics

The glory of the last days

Your hearts will be under attack that you will display a negative attitude towards Christianity; many will Misquote God and Jesus to continue living in their transgressions. Love will be dethroned from the throne of the heart and hate will be the new king to rule over. Through king hate; the rumors of tragic death will spread across and many will live in fear as the world become more unsafe for its inhabitants. Satan will plant the seed of wickedness and our generation will produce evil as a result.

End time ethics

The glory of the last days

Be warned; Jesus is coming very soon, even 20 years from now is too soon for Jesus' return. The time left for his coming maybe too far for you, but as far as he is concerned every time is too soon for him. Blessed are those who hear the word of God and keep it.

End time ethics

Chapter 12

The Time of the End

DANIEL 12 VERSE 1 "At that time shall arise Michael, the great prince who has charge of your people. And there shall be a time of trouble; such as never has been since there was a nation till that time.

But at that time your people shall be delivered, everyone whose name shall be found written in the book. And many of those who sleep in the dust of the earth shall awake, some to everlasting life, and some to shame and everlasting contempt.

The glory of the last days

And those who are wise shall shine like the brightness of the sky above; and those who turn many to righteousness, like the stars forever and ever. But you, Daniel, shut up the words and seal the book, until the time of the end.

Many shall run to and fro, and knowledge shall increase." Then I, Daniel, looked, and behold, two others stood, one on this bank of the stream and one on that bank of the stream.

End time ethics

The glory of the last days

And someone said to the man clothed in linen, who was above the waters of the stream, "How long shall it be till the end of these wonders?" And I heard the man clothed in linen, who was above the waters of the stream; he raised his right hand and his left hand toward heaven and swore by him who lives forever that it would be for a time, times, and half a time, and that when the shattering of the power of the holy people comes to an end all these things would be finished.

End time ethics

The glory of the last days

I heard, but I did not understand. Then I said, "O my lord, what shall be the outcome of these things?" He said, "Go your way, Daniel, for the words are shut up and sealed until the time of the end. Many shall purify themselves and make themselves white and be refined, but the wicked shall act wickedly.

And none of the wicked shall understand, but those who are wise shall understand. And from the time that the regular burnt offering is taken away and the abomination that makes desolate is set up, there shall be 1,290 days. Blessed is he who waits and arrives at the 1,335 days. But go your way till the end. And you shall rest and shall stand in your allotted place at the end of the days.

End time ethics

The glory of the last days

The sins and doom of ungodly people

"3 My dear friends, I was doing my best to write to you about the salvation we share in common, when I felt the need of writing at once to encourage you to fight on for the faith which once and for all God has given to his people.

4 For some godless people have slipped in unnoticed among us, persons who distort the message about the grace of our God in order to excuse their immoral ways, and who reject Jesus Christ, our only Master and Lord.

End time ethics

The glory of the last days

Long ago the Scriptures predicted the condemnation they have received.

5 For even though you know all this, I want to remind you of how the Lord once rescued the people of Israel from Egypt, but afterward destroyed those who did not believe.

6 Remember the angels who did not stay within the limits of their proper authority, but abandoned their own dwelling place: they are bound with eternal chains in the darkness below, where God is keeping them for that great Day on which they will be condemned.

End time ethics

The glory of the last days

7 Remember Sodom and Gomorrah, and the nearby towns, whose people acted as those angels did and indulged in sexual immorality and perversion: they suffer the punishment of eternal fire as a plain warning to all.

8 In the same way also, these people have visions which make them sin against their own bodies; they despise God's authority and insult the glorious beings above.

End time ethics

The glory of the last days

9 Not even the chief angel Michael did this. In his quarrel with the Devil, when they argued about who would have the body of Moses, Michael did not dare condemn the Devil with insulting words, but said, "The Lord rebuke you!"

10 But these people attack with insults anything they do not understand; and those things that they know by instinct, like wild animals, are the very things that destroy them.

11 How terrible for them! They have followed the way that Cain took. For the sake of money they have given themselves over to the error that Balaam committed.

End time ethics

The glory of the last days

They have rebelled as Korah rebelled, and like him they are destroyed. 12 With their shameless carousing they are like dirty spots in your fellowship meals. They take care only of themselves.

They are like clouds carried along by the wind, but bringing no rain. They are like trees that bear no fruit, even in autumn, trees that have been pulled up by the roots and are completely dead.

13 They are like wild waves of the sea, with their shameful deeds showing up like foam. They are like wandering stars, for whom God has reserved a place forever in the deepest darkness.

End time ethics

The glory of the last days

14 It was Enoch, the seventh direct descendant from Adam, who long ago prophesied this about them: "The Lord will come with many thousands of his holy angels 15 to bring judgment on all, to condemn them all for the godless deeds they have performed and for all the terrible words that godless sinners have spoken against him!"

16 These people are always grumbling and blaming others; they follow their own evil desires; they brag about themselves and flatter others in order to get their own way.

End time ethics

The glory of the last days

Warnings and Instructions

17 But remember, my friends, what you were told in the past by the apostles of our Lord Jesus Christ. 18 They said to you, "When the last days come, people will appear who will make fun of you, people who follow their own godless desires."

19 These are the people who cause divisions, who are controlled by their natural desires, who do not have the Spirit. 20 But you, my friends, keep on building yourselves up on your most sacred faith. Pray in the power of the Holy Spirit,

End time ethics

The glory of the last days

21 and keep yourselves in the love of God, as you wait for our Lord Jesus Christ in his mercy to give you eternal life.

22 Show mercy toward those who have doubts; 23 save others by snatching them out of the fire; and to others show mercy mixed with fear, but hate their very clothes, stained by their sinful lusts.

End time ethics

A call to persevere

Perseverance is a mark of every true believer. Jesus said" be faithful even at the point of death, and he also said "whoever persevere these hard times till the end will be given authority to eat on the tree of life",. ....Therefore, among God's churches we boast about your perseverance and faith in all the persecutions and trials you are enduring. (2 Thessalonians 1 verse 4)......Not only so, but we also glory in our sufferings, because we know that suffering produces perseverance; 4 perseverance, character; and character, hope.

The glory of the last days

5 And hope does not put us to shame, because God's love has been poured out into our hearts through the Holy Spirit, who has been given to us. (Romans 5 verse 3). We have confidence in the Lord that you are doing and will continue to do the things we command. 5 May the Lord direct your hearts into God's love and Christ's perseverance. (2 Thessalonians 3 verse 5)

Surrounded by such a great cloud of witnesses, let us throw off everything that hinders and the sin that so easily entangles.

End time ethics

The glory of the last days

And let us run with perseverance the race marked out for us, 2 fixing our eyes on Jesus, the pioneer and perfecter of faith. For the joy set before him he endured the cross, scorning its shame, and sat down at the right hand of the throne of God.

3 Consider him who endured such opposition from sinners, so that you will not grow weary and lose heart. (Hebrews 12 verse 1).Consider it pure joy, my brothers and sisters, whenever you face trials of many kinds, 3 because you know that the testing of your faith produces perseverance.

The glory of the last days

4 Let perseverance finish its work so that you may be mature and complete, not lacking anything. (James 1 verse 3).

Brothers and sisters, as an example of patience in the face of suffering, take the prophets who spoke in the name of the Lord.

11 As you know, we count as blessed those who have persevered. You have heard of Job's perseverance and have seen what the Lord finally brought about. The Lord is full of compassion and mercy.

End time ethics

The glory of the last days

(James 5 verse 11)......... For this very reason, make every effort to add to your faith goodness; and to goodness, knowledge; 6 and to knowledge, self-control; and to self-control, perseverance; and to perseverance, godliness; 7 and to godliness, mutual affection; and to mutual affection, love. 8 For if you possess these qualities in increasing measure, they will keep you from being ineffective and unproductive in your knowledge of our Lord Jesus Christ.

End time ethics

9 But whoever does not have them is nearsighted and blind, forgetting that they have been cleansed from their past sins. (2peter 1 verse 6).

TO GOD BE THE GLORY

AMEN

ABOUT THE AUTHOR

Vusi Mxolisi Zitha is always been known by his virtue of honesty and integrity. His educational background in Nature Conservation includes writing of reports, articles and conducting field research. In 2009 he was involved in a Road Safety school debate under the motion: "Public transport and infrastructures are now ready for the 2010 FIFA world cup".

He got a certificate of achievement from the road safety department having been successfully defeating over nine schools contesting.
His scholastic contextual in nature conservation and debate has given him a

End time ethics

broad base from which to approach many topics.

Vusi has also served as a youth leader in the Church of God of Prophecy for over nine years. He also conducted several sermons and hosted youth services in the church as a junior pastor under the endorsement of District overseer Mr. Harry Mpumelelo Mavuso. His first book (Each step serves a purpose) is an inspirational, motivational and courageous book based on life encounters.

Other books by: Vusi Mxolisi Zitha

1. Each step serves a purpose

2. The realities of life

3. Exaltations to God

4. The book of proverbs

5. wise sayings

6. Eternity is the righteous only inheritance

7. Hell is the agony of the wicked

8. The glory of the last days

9. The book of parables

End time ethics

The glory of the last days

To get them type the book title on;

www.amazon.com

www.goodreads.com

www.smashwords.com

www.abebooks.com

www.kobowritinglife.com

www.powells.com

www.thriftbook.com

www.saxo.com

www.mightyape.co.nz

End time ethics

The glory of the last days

Connect with me on:

Social

https://m.facebook.com/vusi.mxolisi.75

https://www.instagram.com/vusi.mxolisi/

https://www.linkedin.com/in/vusi-mxolisi-zitha/

Web:

www.vusimxolisi.wordpress.com

http://vusimxolisi.tumblr.com/

Author page:

www.amazon.com//e/BO7YLVVW59

End time ethics

The glory of the last days

For quotes, sayings proverbs and inspirational stories

https://www.mirakee.com/vusimxolisizitha

https://www.yourquote.in/vusi-mxolisi-zitha-bqhjd/quotes

https://www.allchristianquotes.org/profile/user/2127/vusi_mxolisi_zitha/

https://www.wattpad.com/user/vusimxolisi

https://www.pinterest.com.mx/vusimxolisi/

For blogs

https://www.vusimxolisizitha.blogspot.com

https://www.goodreads.com/author_blog_posts/

https://www.vusimxolisi.wordpress.com/blog/

End time ethics

The glory of the last days

The glory of the last days

End time ethics

The glory of the last days

End time ethics

www.ingramcontent.com/pod-product-compliance
Lightning Source LLC
Chambersburg PA
CBHW081358160426
43193CB00013B/2058